Winter

Published in Great Britain in 2024
by Big White Shed, Morecambe, Lancashire
www.bigwhiteshed.co.uk
Printed and bound by Imprint Digital, Devon

ISBN 978-1-915021-37-3
Copyright © Big White Shed
Cover Design by Robert Lever @leverart

The rights of the individuals to be identified as authors of this work has been asserted in their accordance with Copyright, Designs and Patents Act of 1988, all rights reserved.

A CIP catalogue record of this book is available from the British Library.

wrap yourself in winter
let the words warm you

Contents

Hedge Witch..6
charm for inspiration..7
Oriented Away...8
Autumn Excavation..10
Aurora Borealis Over England..11
Northern Lights..12
On the Platform...13
Winter, the uninvited but not entirely unwelcome house guest...................14
When in Winter...16
Season's Grittings..18
The Moss Poem...20
Looking In...22
Shining Star...23

Christmas Dinner	24
Pescatarian Christmas	25
Christmas Circus	26
Xmas	27
You Contain Multitudes	28
across the glass	30
Dragon	31
A Middle Aged Woman's New Year's Resolutions	32
Beginnings	34
The Uncertainty of Snow	36
Fairy Lights	38
Last Month of Winter	39
The Breath of Hope	40
Waiting for Spring	41

Hedge Witch

The hedge-witch
starts her striptease,
a slow reveal.
Bronze days
torn and tattered
by long dry
blackthorn fingers.
Shredded cloth of gold,
echoes of summer cling.
Wild as the wind
she dances,
barefoot.
Brazenly,
bringing winter
in her wake.

Sue Allen

charm for inspiration

a cowslip picked by winter's light
green nettles blanched to soothe the bite

marsh mallow crushed for all its worth
calendula plucked from the earth

rosehips picked and pressed and dried
and samphire smoothed by time and tide

a spider's web all pricked with pins
a spell to wake the soul within

to help the tongue re-learn to sing
to make the body yearn for wings

Leanne Moden

Oriented Away

Coated in the last of the leaves
blown back against walls
old sun hides.
Air takes flesh,
stiffens itself
over car windows, up pipes,
twists tarmac still hurt
from last year's visit.
Inside again
twines like a cat round Mr Braithwaite's fire,
listening out for more
of its own language. Gap between

door and road widens.
Where roads lead and why
is uncertain.
Even the thickest woolly sweater
seems to shiver
and turn away.
It doesn't help that it's
happened umpteen times before
this clumping,
sky-blue calcified to grit,
to grey-slate. Breath revealed
leans in, observes itself gain density,

a silver-seed swan
caught where water
is sharp and pressing
worth the remembering
to the deep-minded earth.

Kevin Qweaver Jackson

Autumn Excavation

Tease out silver grey jumper, released
from summer's build-up of sun tops and shorts.
Bright and balmy days lie behind,
dark, damp future calls for tee shirts in layers,
bright blue waterproof casing.

Rivers overflow, traffic builds up
exhaust fumes invade road-side homes. Bright lights,
red, green, gold, swing dejected in the damp
invasive wind. No deep and crisp and even
for us, but a faithful, grey jumper
growing itchier every year.

Helen Sadler

Aurora Borealis Over England

The sky thinks it is Christmas, has dragged out
multi-coloured fairy lights, red, gold, blue,
strung stars across night's darkness. We all shout,
See the northern stars' twinkling silver hues.

No-one wants to go inside. We bear frost,
ignore icy air just to see lollipops,
swirls of white candy, red and green stripes lost,
hanging like treats on a tree, gems, gumdrops.

Ethereal colours soothe tired eyes
and we see some magic, a lost kingdom.
Santa is coming with his surprise –
for now we have sparkle, nature's wisdom,

tinsel strands hanging, catching the bright lights,
energy charged. We look on in pure delight.

Gail Webb

Northern Lights

Sat in the dark trying to see the Northern
Lights, going from room to room on either side
of my house. Feeling kind of stupid now. Feeling
left out. I missed them once before, woke up
in the morning to a feed full of wriggling
candyfloss. If I tilt – if I'm squinting – I trick myself
into thinking maybe the sky's a little more pink on
the horizon than usual – or something? It's like the time
I kept looking away from the storm and that's when
everyone else saw the fork lightning. Nature's having a party
and I'm not invited. But sometimes, I see rainbows
when I'm lost or indecisive, and that's how I know
even when I'm alone, the rhythm and the flow
of the universe is listening and sure, maybe tonight
I won't see the Northern Lights – I'm on the wrong side
of the city where the sky is too bright – but
I can hear my cats purring as they follow me around
from room to room, from side to side of my house.
Isn't that a little miracle in its own right?

Thom Seddon

On the Platform

The fog hasn't quite dissipated. The world
is soaked in a white, creamy light, awaiting
the sunshine to take over. The booming
locomotives sound strangely soothing,
interrupted by repetitive announcements
of *See it. Say it. Sorted.* The chill wind cuts
my cheeks and numbs my nose from the dizzy
smell of the diesel. I bury myself under thick
layers of clothes and a scarf, fingertips
squeezing the air trapped inside the gloves.

The thought of snow leaps into mind:
a snow that is neither too heavy nor
too light, like the one we had last Christmas,
when red jumpers and silver ribbons joined
hands to expel the lingering gloom
of the year, ending months of waiting
and miles of yearning. Your smile, soaked
red in mulled wine, reminds me that joy
is always too brief and too intoxicating.
       At least we'll see each other soon.

Hongwei Bao

Winter, the uninvited
     but not entirely unwelcome house guest

You've known she was coming for months but
her lack of clarity of when she's coming or going,
leaves you not knowing whether you're coming or going.
But there's always enough time for a bit of a clean-up as she makes you see your home with fresh eyes, if not fresh paint. You regret those wasted summer months but you know deep down there are no such things.

And then she arrives
in the middle of the night,
banging on your door, rattling your windows, an unpaid taxi with radio blaring.

She knows the value of good luggage and has packed, in no particular order: calmness, danger, juniper gin, a skeleton of truth, unfathomable beauty, a half-eaten packet of Bourbon creams, predictable unpredictability, holly berries and a pack of playing cards she won from a shirtless sailor in the port of Athens. She may not need the Bourbons.

She remains in your top four list of friends, but she is forever texting other friends, the ever-growing masses of the Storm Crew, endlessly adding new names to her list of contacts. Barbara and Eunice seem to be her current faves. She demands the heating on at all hours and she spends an age in the shower, just long enough for her conscience to be cleaned of not spending anything at all on the heating and shower bills.

One night she decides to rearrange your garden, throws new shapes with the furniture, pulls up trees and fences, encouraging conversations with neighbours. In the middle of her stay she wants parties – two in a week at which she'll work through wish lists, scratch cards, ex-lovers and resolutions. She's formed a WhatsApp group with the Storm Crew. And after the parties you're flat as a pancake until the pancakes come out. Six weeks of endless darkness, early nights, dwindling resources.

But one morning, in the midst of the mists, you lie on her bed ("her bed!?") and watch her applying make-up. She's hungover after a night on hand plucked tiles, decrying the Old Masters, the old Turners and old Constables and their failure to never quite capture her good side. She then recalls a young constable who did manage to capture her backside and how she doesn't return his texts. She piles on powder and glitter to complement the pinks and reds and blues of her early morning eyes and skies. And you remember why you loved her in your youth but didn't even know it at the time.

She coaxes you out for a walk and makes you see her home with fresh eyes, that low heatless sunshine bringing new clarity, new definitions to memories and sights, your fire on one bar, your pilot light still lit.

When she leaves, you're not sure if she's really left at all, she's left that much behind, her nail varnish, her toothbrush, her broken spines. She pops back a couple of times to remind you of her hold. Like all the best pain, grief and stress, when's she gone, you can't quite recall her touch and her power. She'll return roughly the same time next year, no firm dates offered. She's gone back packing in Australia. At her age. She pins a lipstick-stained Greek Queen of Clubs to your bedhead and leaves you exhausted and refreshed in equal measures, and ever-more determined to decorate before Spring stays over.

Keith Ford

When in Winter

When I'm scuffing
shards of snow,
scraping, shuffling,
slither, slither,
shape to skid,

I'll think of you.

Buttoning coats,
with red raw fingers,
shielding flesh,
shiver, shiver,
under cloth,

you'll be there.

When cupping milk
straight from boiling,
wrap around,
wrap around,
ruddy hands.

When rays of yellow
light, from houses,
decorates the damp,
worn streets
of season.

When I'm burning logs,
watching flames rise,
and taking the radio
to soft sheets,

when in winter,

I'll think of you.

Chris Towers

Season's Grittings

You know the summer's over when
the clocks go back, the geese take flight
eleven takes the place of ten
and the council's email starts again.

As autumn follows summer's end
the heating's on, the leaves blaze bright.
It's great to see this good old friend
when freezing weather might impend.

It's so comforting to know
the gritter's going out tonight
to salt our crunchy roads despite
the winter's freezing undertow.

When expecting ice or frost or snow
the RST's the thing to know
impress your friends with its precision
ignore their ill-informed derision.

That your gritting email warms your heart
with nerdy joy is all that counts
you'll know the data it imparts
as festival excitement mounts.

This started as a villanelle
but the rhyming quickly slipped and fell
my path of words had not been gritted
I've lost the pattern, bloody hell

most inconvenient in the middle
of our lovely frozen winter idyll
let's get this ditty back on track,
be cheerful, positive, laid back...

We are so glad that winter's here!
For Christmas shopping's sheer delight!
for songs of seasonal festive cheer!
can't wait for more of this next year!

At home by firelight's golden glow
there are carols on the radio
and in the slowly dwindling light
we kiss beneath the mistletoe.

Vron McIntyre

(RST = road surface temperature)

The Moss Poem

(I wrote you most days from the rainforest floor)

                                                                 This is where the
                                                                      moss was
                                                                   and they were too

I am out of touch and missing all at once
unable to get back to the surface
swimming next to a blue flame
glowing ectoplasm glitters
the tour guide is a woman's voice   under the stars
everything concave is inside out   far away from what it once was,
                                                                                                  un-inverted

happy is the uncertain   I looked for you in the chrysalis
and you

                                                                    were still wearing
                                                                        your socks
                                                                 when you disappeared
I found them in my drawer three days later   tucked themselves in
still covered in glitter from the caves
I had so many questions when I reached out my hands
stuck to the walls and swallowed my palm

                                                       silicone and retreating light
it wanted me to stay in a time I could only help but leave
the artist gold leafed my throat like it was delicate

ready to go on stage   wearing shoe covers
walking and talking   gently avoiding   swinging their arms
the foxgloves developed negatives backwards
in gelatine   over water
pasted down   every darkness bright green lime green
stinging   immediately nauseous
turning to stone   under the gaze of the walls.

Jodie Whitchurch

Looking In

I hop off the bus and head home, feeling tired and hungry. I slow my footsteps. The road is deserted, apart from cars neatly parked on both sides. All the houses look full and busy. Lights on. Too many.

Colourful lights decorating the magnolia trees and holly bushes in the front gardens remind me that it's Christmas. Not a holiday I usually celebrate, yet away from my family in China, looking into the brightly lit windows, I can't help being drawn to the festive atmosphere.

Inside one window stands a big, camel-like reindeer with a red nose. Inside another a woman is peeling potatoes on the kitchen worktop. Inside another, silhouettes are moving, as if dancing, or playing a game.

A warm feeling rises in me, and I feel a sudden throb in my heart. Perhaps it's the cold wind. Perhaps it's the smoke from the burning wood in the air. Perhaps it's a feeling of joy. Until I realise that I'm the only person walking on the street, looking into other people's lives, watching their happiness.

Hongwei Bao

✱

You're

my shining star
So beautiful, but so far

I wish you Merry Christmas
bigger than miles between us.

All the presents under all the trees
are not as many as you mean to me

I'd swap the excitement of every Santa visit
to be with you today and share the Christmas magic.

Love

From

Me x

Vicky Pealing

Christmas Dinner

Not a voyeur, but I did stare at the pixels of your life.
Intrusive:
Stayed longer than comfortable, your guests arrived.
You prompted them to say hello to my virtual eyes.
They pointed and laughed with awkward smiles.
I'm certain you forgot I was there. Forgotten.
I tried to catch your sight to say, "I should go,"
oblivious, you said the bird cooked slow.
Watching a farce, a very bad show.
Heart smoking and broken.
"Sit, eat, please tuck in."
"I should be going."
Only 1 knowing
how lonely
a video
call can
be.

Vicky Pealing

A Pescatarian Christmas

Nobody wants Wolf round for Christmas
The media's done a proper job on him
> *He'll blow down your house, then eat up your pets.*

The outlook they painted was grim.
But we read books, not tabloid papers
We know Wolf's misunderstood and alone
> *You're welcome here, but we're pescatarian*
> *You might want to bring meaty food of your own.*

So Wolf turned up, buzzing with excitement
Wiping paws at the door as he'd been taught by his pack.
He'd brought some gifts and goodies
In a hamper slung across his back.
He pulled out a box filled with pizzas
Paraded it round the room with glee
> *I'm so very grateful to be sharing today with you*
> *So I made one of the pizzas with anchovies!*

Anne Holloway

Christmas Circus

let today be all glitter and chatter
breathe in the scent of needles
                       drop*p*ing
set the fairy-lights to *twinkle*
from c-h-a-s-e
dab on the perfume
that makes you sneeze
squeeeze into that dress
in the size you used to be
leaf through the book
by that woman you **loathe**
tuck your feet into comedy slippers.
Allow the paper hat
to slip
       pour a glass of
something
crack a walnut
if you can
unwrap a sweet

       keep the circus out
it will leave its mark
but the grass
will grow back
like it's never been

Anne Holloway

Xmas

electric menorah in the window   nine orange bulbs all set to glow   middle one called the shamash   lights the others   I'm craving different colours   neighbour's bushes blink   blue green red   santa's hands on his big belly   pom pom hat   vermillion   at least tonight we'll go inside   xmas eve we're all invited   pine cone wreath on neighbours door   reindeer antlers on fox labrador living room decked out   red silver green   pine tree nearly hits the ceiling   we have trees like that as well but no candy canes and tinsel   they stand outside in front of the drive   not dressed up   so deprived   sit crossed legged on the floor   with sisters I have met before ursula and heidi wear scarlet velvet   with long blonde braids and gold barrettes   munch sugar cookies shaped like stars   smell of cinnamon everywhere   later when everyone's asleep   put on my dressing gown   carnation pink   creep downstairs unscrew the shamash   stuff in the pocket of my pyjamas   orange is not my favourite colour   sneak out the door to my neighbours   borrow one red light from a twinkling bush   wonder if anyone will notice

Beverly Frydman

You Contain Multitudes

you are red rosebuds, orange stones
a coil of copper wire

> pink five-lobed spring flowers
> strutting flamingoes

you are sunflowers in a basket
a swarm of bees

> teardrops, snowflakes
> fireflies in a jar

you are many yellow suns
sliced lemons and limes

> a string of garden strawberries
> glittering magenta spheres.

you are a starburst of white filaments
a string of pearls

> planets and icicles
> candle flames flickering.

you are moonbeams and starshine
shimmering nets of blue

>   twisting yellow vines
>   an entanglement of ivy

you are pine cones, and acorns
fly agaric mushrooms

>   spiders' webs, flying ghosts
>   golden autumn leaves

you are the bluest of eyeballs
a dance of purple skeletons

>   a forest of arced rainbows
>   a curtain of tiny twinkles

you are antlered elk and snowmen
ribbons and footballs

>   campervans and christmas trees
>   parcels and pears

you are apples and pumpkins
oil lamps and maple leaves

you are chili peppers
you are chinese lanterns
you are lions&tigers&bears

Vron McIntyre

across the glass
(stoke to manchester train journey)

fog wears many masks - to hide its world beneath
snow drives - shaves the ground (makes the whiskers blue)
fog's cleaner sister - frost - bites us with its teeth
morning with its grimace maps into the proof

snow drives - shaves the ground (makes the whiskers blue)
fog's better out than in - and watched behind the glass
january (at last) blows colder in its brew
we watch the landscape alter in its pass

fog's cleaner sister - frost - bites us with its teeth
we check our list - scarves - hats - dry socks - flasks
the old year dead - we served it with a wreath
we marvel at how the chill has hit the grass

morning in its grimace maps into the proof
snow's drift shaved the ground (turned the whiskers blue)

Dave Wood

Dragon

I am dragon as the year dies,
cold morning takes breath to smoke,
as fire stumbles past my teeth
and burns the gossamer air.
I am hoarding
filling my lair with treasures
stolen from the world.
Memories and plans
hands chapped to scales
wings and tail swung on shoulders
from a hook by the door
ready to fly on two legs.
Scarce winter cannot hinder.
I am the creature from stories
endured on page, scroll and tongue
burnt my tracks with heatless feet,
through frost or snow.
Through long nights and old tales
as the night draws in
when words are their most powerful
I tell myself,
Once Upon a Time.
Then again.
Then again.

Ben Macpherson

A Middle Aged Woman's New Year's Resolutions

The sensibilities have a way of placing you
somewhere,
different.

When the man in the restaurant
talks to me of pensions
and stocks and shares
of aches and pains
and mortgages and poverty
I understand
I am his age,
I too wear glasses.

And when we talk of dreams
and love
and touching the sides of life
still
now.

I am not saying
you should leave anyone.
I just know

that the difference
between hanging in that tree and me is

breathing the air
on a January day.

Falling off my stool, twice
drunk,
and looking at someone
anyone, with love.

So I intend fully
to kiss that woman
on her lips
and flirt with the man next door.

To sniff something
I have never sniffed before,
and to lie down in front of someone
who may not want me.

To soak my feet because they hurt
and late at night, drink
hot chocolate.

Cathy Symes

Beginnings

January is the coldest month, sleeping
late in my warm bed, forgetting
fresh new resolutions, watching
for the high wolf moon, walking
in low red sun. Freezing
roots un-watered by showers. Slithering
on ice the webbed-feet ducks.

With no shower of rain, I stopped by the frozen lake,
and went on in sunlight, into the courtyard
and drank hot chocolate and tried to write
for an hour.
Assaulted by cold, I walked on, seeking,
a poet-pilgrim.

The beginning of the calendar.
The beginning of lengthening days.
The beginning of nothing.

We wait for the real beginning.
Buds, fattening roots, blossom,
lilacs, hyacinths.
And freedom –

Ready to wend on my pilgrimage, leaving
the mask at home
the lateral flow test
the aching news.
A seeking of strange lands
And a blessing on those who helped
when we were sick.

Clare Stewart

The Uncertainty of Snow

You can't grasp the last month of winter,
cold climate compresses reason, eludes touch.

Should it be February, or maybe March will snow this year?
Ask Mother, she knows best, or did... but then ghosts... they know

of the longing for the past, the masks we wear,
the need to care... where all this goes when loved ones ... go.

Maybe my others will understand if I seem absent,
and follow only the scent of when I was more certain in the world.

I say hello to the past, lift the lid of the box, stare at yesterday,
wonder why it seems visceral, bloody-lovely-ugly real.

The things we put in boxes, of memory and toxins,
with a healthy dose of rose-tinted love,

which is the thing that draws us back each time,
the warmth of arms holding in heat, holding in heart,

never mind we know the emptiness of departing, the bare branches
of hurting, shedding skin to acknowledge all that ending.

Holding our bodies like urns,
we turn our backs, scatter the present as ash.

I lift the box lid again, just to check everything's there,
where I left it, neatly folded, placed.

When did you say it was Mother, the last month of winter,
February or March?

Or did you say it's something we never really know,
left to the uncertainty of snow.

John Humphreys

Fairy Lights

It's their unreliability
which reminds me.
Not of you,
but the feeling I had
when we were together.
That I said was like
the glow which surrounded the
streetlight in the mornings.
The one by the entrance to the park,
where I wondered if it was the bulb,
but you said it was just the reflection
against the wall. Flickering back at us.
Through the mist.
On and off.
On and off.
On and off.

Cathy Symes

Last Month of Winter

she visits her father each day
squeezes his hand
coaxes him to sip water
he smiles
the carers hug her when she leaves
as if they are waiting for it to end
as if winter is a bad thing
as if a hoar frost is less beautiful
than cherry blossom
or a field of corn

Anne Holloway

The Breath of Hope

In mid-February it snowed for the second time
and took the breath of hope from us
as we drifted, further.

The Fatsia in the garden drooped, defeated
ice clinging to the tips of its evergreen leaves
sipping lesions onto the ground below.

In the morning the sky was lighter,
earlier, carrying as it does this year
more red raw sorrow than we can remember.

Yet the earth still thawed around us
leaving muddy tracks where sledges ran
through last year's sloping lawns.

Forcing us to wonder.
What was lost.
What will remain.

Cathy Symes

Waiting for Spring

there are no flowers
the earth is painting new ones
deep below the soil

Michelle Mother Hubbard

Many thanks to the poets who have kindly offered their poems for inclusion in this book. Big White Shed isn't just a publishing press, we are a community of folks who believe in the power of words.

Kevin Qweaver Jackson	Michelle Mother Hubbard
Sue Allen	Leanne Moden
Helen Sadler	Gail Webb
Thom Seddon	Hongwei Bao
Keith Ford	Chris Towers
Vron McIntyre	Jodie Whitchurch
Vicky Pealing	Anne Holloway
Beverly Frydman	Dave Wood
Ben Macpherson	Cathy Symes
Clare Stewart	John Humphreys

Please keep in touch, and if you like what we do, buy our books!
You can reach any of the poets by contacting us
www.bigwhiteshed.co.uk
@bigwhiteshed